poems for heartbreak

E.S. Higgins

Copyright © 2022 Peanut Prints
All rights reserved.
ISBN: 978-0-6485460-5-4

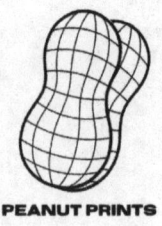

PEANUT PRINTS

How could you explain heartbreak to a child

Whose mind is pure and simple

How could you describe internal pain

To a wide smile with deep dimples

A child would tell you that if you love someone, you should tell them and that's that

But how could you explain to a child that the person you love doesn't love you back.

The coming of the end

Days of happiness have fallen to uncertainty

You start to question everything you've said

There's something different now

Something wrong

You think that it's something you've done

Yawning silence and painful cringes

Entire days consumed with by the thought of them

You think maybe you're being crazy so you dismiss those feelings

But you know deep down that you are right.

Whole days consumed by the thought of them

You try to distract yourself but you can't

It feels as though you're looking through a looking glass

At memories that are long gone

You feel unworthy

Not good enough

Your mind goes in circles

As you torture yourself in silence.

Distance doesn't have to be physical

You could hold it in your arms

You could kiss it and tell it you love it

And yet it's never been greater before

You can feel it in your heart

The empty pain

That comes after heartbreak

Knowing that things will never be the same.

You think of how it used to be

Long days of laughter

Smiling at one another and giggling

Staring into each other's eyes as you lay in silence

You remember how it used to be

All just memories now

That you look back on in painful silence.

When you hit rock bottom

And all you can feel is the beating of your heart

As pain gnaws at your insides

You don't care about anything anymore

You'd throw it all away

Just for another day

Laughing in the sunlight with them.

Finally, the day has come

Where you know that you're going to break up

And even though you're still in love

The person you love is ready to move on

Your body shakes in misery

Ready for the pain to come

But you could never be ready enough

When you realise that someone you love is gone.

That night you barely sleep

Tossing and turning in misery

Playing the final moments on repeat

Reading over messages you've already seen

You see them in your dreams

But you wake up alone

You roll over and check your phone

Half hoping to see a message

But you don't.

The first day of being alone

You're constantly checking your phone

Still in shock the pain hasn't set in

You call your friends and let them in

Into everything that you're feeling

They tell you that they're sorry and that they're there if you need

You know they are but at night you see

That at the end of the day you are alone

You roll over in bed and check your phone.

A week passes but every day feels the same

Blasting music to try and mute the pain

Your insides feel detached and all you can think of is them

You wonder if they've moved on yet

Your mind races as you think the worst

You distract yourself but you still hurt

You turn the music up louder and try to chase it away

But music mixes with pain.

Nobody cares about nice guys

They care about bad guys who can be nice.

Self-loathing

You don't like who you are

Clearly, you're not good enough

Riddled with jealousy and insecurity

You look at other people and your stomach drops

You wonder if that's the kind of person they're looking for

A week of silence

Consumed by thoughts

Of how you are not good enough.

Is there a wasteland

Where the broken hearts go to grieve

Tormented by raging storms and cracks of lightning

Thick clouds that cast the land in eternal twilight

Is that where the broken hearts go?

To feel repent for what they know they deserve

Lost and alone

It's a long journey home

From where the broken hearts go.

No more messages on your phone

You keep checking it though

You refresh it over and over again

And fight the urge to write one to send

You know that it would do no good

But just to get a response you would

Write anything just to see the reply

As you sit in silence and wonder why.

At a party

Your body is there but your mind is far away

You're laughing and talking but you can't wait

To leave and go home where you can be at ease

In the silence of your room where you can try and pick up the pieces.

How could someone be dead to us but still alive

You send a message with no reply

How could your heart love something that doesn't love it back?

Something with so much depth can't understand

That some things were never meant to be

The sooner you realise that the sooner you'll be free.

Social media is the jailor of broken hearts

Reminding them of just how lonely they are

Breaking more as they scroll down the news feed

Terrified of what they might see

That person that they're looking for

Looks much happier than they did before

The room is dark but the phone screen is bright

As the jailor torments its prisoner all night.

Back again

In a place you know

The place you fall to when you're feeling high

Back again

To where you're low

You stop and wonder why

You come here time after time

Why you miss it when you're gone

Back again

You wonder where it all went wrong.

I was trying to play the game

But my bluff got pulled

I spilled the beans all over myself

I put it all on the line

My heart skipped a beat

The yawning gap between you and me

Makes my spirit mourn.

Everyone has baggage

That they pull around with them like wet clothes

Baggage blocks our ears

And makes us deaf to the songs of love

Sung from a heart that's been broken many times before

But ready to let it all go.

A little tree watched the world go by

Atop a hill somewhere in the country side

Through rain and storm

On sunny days and lonely nights

The tree watched the world go by

It watched the grass turn green in the springtime

Only to wither again and die

Its own leaves fell from its branches and grew back

Time and time again

And as much grief it felt for the falling leaves

It felt joy again when they returned

And all was in balance.

The ghost of our ex's

Follow us around on our phones

Old messages from them

You read back over when you're alone

You try to make sense of it all

Where did it all go wrong

You think it was you

Although it was probably something in them all along

While the skeletons try and break out of the closet

Tears fall down your cheeks like water from a faucet

There is no shame in feeling pain

No sense trying to ignore the rain

To feel it all is what life is for

And then you build upon it all

To forge yourself into who you were always meant to be

Sometimes it just takes a heartbreak to see.

Physical pain starts to heal right away

Emotional pain changes depending on the day

Ups and downs while you get tortured silently by your mind

Aching for someone who left you behind.

Slowly you begin to feel better about yourself

Being with friends and good music always helps

And although you still feel the aching pain

Not every day feels the same

Your laughter is a little more genuine

Cracking at the casket of ice around your heart

Slowly you start to remember

What an amazing person you are.

When you look out into the horizon

You can feel the intense beauty of life

When you lift your face towards the sky

And let yourself get washed and cleansed by the sunlight

Slowly you heal in the hands of nature

No longer in an intense state of deafening misery

But a beautiful state of wistful melancholy

You sit in silence and listen

To the music that's playing softly in your heart.

Left alone

Somewhere under solar beams

You try to find meaning in your life

Sifting through memories

Replaying them over again

Understanding things takes time

Years of silent frustration

Have finally come to an end

When you realise who you are

You no longer feel the pain of having to pretend.

You start to work on your self-doubt

Now that all those tears have leaked out

And even though you're exhausted you pick yourself up

Sometimes there are more important things in life than love

Like appreciating who you are and what you do

And realising that there are very special things about you

You're not worthless and all those things that made you feel pain

You are made of sunlight and rain

A balance of things that come at different times

To feel it all is the meaning of life.

You have to find a way to come to terms with it.

We are amalgamations of thought

Concepts with arms and legs

Blessed with a beating heart

And given a mind that's complex

But all the ideas it creates

Are they really you?

The beauty of life is

Is that one person is made by two.

People who were once in our lives never truly leave our hearts

They become a part of who we are

Tender kisses left upon our cheeks become like battle scars

Faces we think of when we look up in silence at the stars

If you take a deep breath and try to see

That in heartbreak and pain there is beauty

And even though it feels awful it reminds us that we're alive

In happiness and pain our souls are alight.

You are not weak because you don't want to see

Pictures of them on your news feed

You're not crazy because you still think

Of them even though it's been ages since

There are no rules to dealing with pain

No textbooks with step by steps to get through heartbreak

Especially when it comes to self-recovery

Eventually we all come to see

That leaves grow back on bare trees.

Days of uncontrollable anger

Resentment boils as you relapse

Twisting memories over in your head

Everything you've built upon begins to collapse

Sometimes you still can't believe

That those times are all just memoires

That come back to sting you from time to time

On those days when they're the only thing on your mind.

Two people in love

Are still two different people

Together on individual journeys

Walking the same path hand in hand

But some journeys come to forks in the road

And although they may wait for a time, unwilling to leave

It only creates tension

Eventually they have to continue walking

Down separate paths but that was always meant to be

That's just the way it is.

True sadness is in someone who no longer cries.

No one looks like them

No one has their smell

Their laugh and their eyes

No one is like them

The little things that make them special

Can't be easily replaced.

You're worried that you'll never feel love again

At least in the way you did before

That sublime feeling in your heart

Full of excitement

You used to count down the days until you saw them next

You're worried that you'll never feel like that about someone

Like that kind of love is a one-time thing

Caged in by the walls you build around it

You're worried that it'll never climb out again and be free.

A day will come when you see them with someone else.

And although it's the last thing you want right now, one day you'll find someone too.

Everything you see reminds you of them

You feel like you're in a movie

You listen to the soundtrack while you're sitting on the train

Looking out the window you exhale the pain

Somewhere in that city they're walking around too

The difference is they're not thinking about you.

I was drunk in the pub when I thought about you

I was sitting at a table with my friends

I laughed with them but I didn't feel it inside

I knew I shouldn't be thinking about you so I tried

To think of something else but all I could see was your face

That glint you had in your eye on our first date

When we had a picnic in Hyde Park but ended up hiding from the rain

I thought my life would never be the same

But now you're gone and nothing's changed.

Some people we meet in life

We meet at the wrong time

All the stars have to align

In order for love to find

A home between two people

Equal and full of joy

But more often than not

The mistiming has the power to destroy

A tender heart

Cringing and full of pain

It's not your fault

That your timing wasn't the same.

Letting go

You watch them drift away silently

Even though they left long before

You clung on to their memory too long

Spoke to it and made new ones that never happened

It takes all the strength in the world

Just to let someone go

But you know you must.

Find out who you are and master it.

One broken heart is sure to break three more

The decimation of scars that we carry on from before

We are only human

Love is much bigger than us

Travelling through bodies

Until one day we turn to dust.

Droplets of rain

Running down the window sill

The wind is howling outside

The trees are bending

Branches and plastic bags are flying through the air

And everything is grey and dark

You make yourself a cup of tea

Get back into bed and get comfy

And spend the day lost in day dreams.

Every relationship is a lesson.

Love is what life is for.

A sweet melancholy

Over distant mountains that are covered in clouds

There is nothing around for the noise to bounce off of

And everything you say disappears into thin air

Before it has the chance to be heard

Scattered into the universe like dust

That drifts away in the gentle breeze.

You could bring Heaven down to Earth

And have all the angels sing in your choir

You could re-invent yourself entirely

For the soul purpose of feeling desired

You could get fit

Tidy up all those loose bits

You could work your ass of for success

And triumph over every uncertainty and test

You could do it all and become the best person you can be

But eventually you'll have to see

That even after all of that

They're never coming back

And one day you have to accept that.

Listen to good music.

You imagine what you'd say

If you ran into them today

You wonder if it'd change

If suddenly they'd realise it was all one big mistake

You picture your embrace

You're crying in each other arms

That's the cruelty of a broken heart

That shows us visions of things that aren't.

There's magic in everything if you're willing to look.

When you remember you had interests

Passion for things in your life

Suddenly you realise you have time

To work on yourself

To do the things you want to do

It's all part of the process

Of building a stronger you.

The sun and the moon

Are two opposite beings

And for a brief moment

Their combined presence brings

Fire and beauty into the evening sky

That washed the world with golden light

A perfect balance between light and dark

Just the same as the balance of what we are.

Eventually we're thankful for everything.

Never let a heartbreak stop you from putting it all on the line

Life is too short and there's no time

To swallow burning questions deep down where they can't escape

Sooner or later it'll be too late

You may as well ask it

As long as you do it with dignity and respect

There's no point living life with regrets

Especially if it's over something as simple as an answer to a question

And no matter how it goes treat it as a lesson

Life is meant to be followed through with intention.

What else but love

Could make you sing when you're alone

What else but love

Could make you dance while nobody is home

What else but love

Could make you laugh and cry at the same time

What else but love

Could give you memories for life

Love

A language that could never be communicated fully with words

Love

What other feeling is felt across the world?

I wonder if two split paths will ever converge

From the vast darkness of memory two people emerge

The same as they used to be but there's something different

Some small mannerisms in their beings but it makes no difference

Because suddenly they no longer want to be alone

So, they take one another's hands and make the journey home

Along the same path in the end.

There's a reason

Why most songs and art

Are all about love.

There are no 'ones'

There are many

They come at different times

We need them at different stages of life

They fill in our gaps

Teach us lessons on becoming a woman or a man

There are no 'ones'

There are many.

A moment will come

When you are thankful for it all

You feel a swell of happiness within you

You have no idea where they are now

It's been years

But you hope they're happy

Your stomach no longer sinks when you think about them

Because you're happy

Despite all of the heartbreak

Despite all the silence and all the pain

Somehow, you'd still do it all over again

Just to fall in love again.

All things seem to make sense in time

Mysteries unveil themselves one by one as years pass by

Your greatest worries back then now make you smile

And even though you didn't feel happy for the longest while

You understand that it was all worthwhile.

Bitter sweet

When we move on but still look back and smile

At periods of our lives that were full of pain

No longer harmful

Lessons taught and understood

Bitter sweet

When someone that was once the centre of your life

Is a distant memory

Waiting to be visited on rainy days

Bitter sweet memories

Waiting to be replayed.

When you start to understand yourself

Your past will help you grow

There are people's hearts in your roots

Love that only you know

And even if it is no more

It will always be where it was before

In times, frozen back then forever

We can only love when we love together.

One day all despair turns to joy.

Heartbreak forces us to grow

You aren't perfect just the way you are

You're made up of little imperfections

But you shouldn't hate yourself for them

Some people lack what other people have

And the combination of the two make the perfect match

Two lost people come together to create a whole

But who you end up with you'll never know

Until the end.

When you find someone new

And they bring out emotions inside of you

You never thought you'd feel again

Suddenly you're filled with excitement

You can hear the music playing once more

As you sway gently to the notes

Sometimes years and years can pass

You just have to keep hope.

All that heartbreak

All those years of pain

Have moulded you into who you are

You look around and realise how far you've come

How much you've grown

And suddenly it all feels worth it

You smile

And the weight on your shoulders feels a little lighter.

I'll still think of you from time to time

I'll wonder where you are in life

And hopefully by then

We'll be able to be friends

Without any pain

You'd be surprised by what time can change.

The journey to recovery

Is one of the biggest journeys in life

One that has no set rules and no time

It could take you years

Full of longing and tears

But one day you will heal.

You're happy because throughout it all you've changed

You've grown and matured and learned hard lessons along the way

I guess that's what life is for at the end of the day

To feel it all, both love and pain

And at the end of any great journey all we could do is smile

Because pain reminds us that inside of us there is still a child

That dreams and wonders about all things free

Sometimes it just takes heartbreak for us to see.

18 years old I was feeling like a dead weight

Stayed home by myself while my friends went to celebrate

When things went pear shaped I convinced myself that I was a burden

Happy on the outside but my heart was hurting

Watching my mum struggle while I didn't have a job

Used to read and write alone so the pain would stop

And back then all I could seem to see

Was that everyone's lives would be easier without me

When you're young but old enough to see all the people you love sacrifice things for you

And you feel like there isn't anything you can do

Sitting in the passenger seat watching my life fly by passively

Negative mind-sets take everything as a tragedy

But as years have gone by I'm beginning to understand

That I was still a boy back then even though I tried to treat myself like a man

And after years of deep shortcomings I'm starting to forgive

The man who was struggling silently because he was just a kid.

Thanks for reading poems for heartbreak. I'm going through a little of it myself at the minute and hoped that putting the process into words would help not only myself but you as well. I hope if you're going through it, you let yourself feel it all and turn it into something beautiful. The times in our lives with the most growth are usually the most painful and uncomfortable. I hope that after the bitter feeling of pain and rejection passes, you can start to look into yourself and understand what makes you, you, and why that makes you special.

It's taken me years just to realise the importance of doing that, and I guess it'll take the rest of my life to find out the what it all means. But, I hope I find

joy in the process, and I hope you can to.
That's what life is for.
Thanks for all of the support.

E.S. Higgins